www.stirredcreations.com

Copyright © Daisy Sud
All rights reserved.
No part of this book may be reproduced or used in any manner without the written
permission of the copyright owner, except for the use of quotations in a book review.
First printing edition 2020.
ISBN: 978-1-7348461-2-6
A delicious concoction of Stirred Creations.

The Color of You & Me
By Daisy Sud

In the beginning, the color of our skin was picked out for you and me.

So many shades of colors to choose, but this one on my skin, I can definitely agree!

You and me are perfectly painted.

We are different,
but the same.

United as one human race,

I'm proud of what we became.

Like the trees in fall, our beauty shines best when our colors are together.

Like puzzle pieces, our shapes can fit neatly next to one another.

I see my color when reaching for food.

It makes me feel like a tasty treat!

We are growing like flowers in bloom.

Regardless of your shape, size, or color—

on a scale, we are all equal.

We're creations made by the best artist, admiring what's on the easel.

So please be kind to all, and every color that you see, because nothing is more perfect than

the color of you and me.

Lightning Source UK Ltd.
Milton Keynes UK
UKRC010748060920
369229UK00005B/4